Original title:
Nectar Notes

Copyright © 2025 Creative Arts Management OÜ
All rights reserved.

Author: Julian Prescott
ISBN HARDBACK: 978-1-80566-755-1
ISBN PAPERBACK: 978-1-80566-825-1

The Taste of Dawn's Embrace

Morning light on toast,
A splash of silly jam.
The taste of dawn's delight,
Like a giggling clam.

Syrup drips and flows,
While pancakes dance away.
A syrupy sorcery,
Makes breakfast a play.

Honeyed Whispers of Bliss

Buzzing bees hum tunes,
In a frothy little hive.
Honey on my spoon,
Makes pancakes come alive.

Sipping sweet sunshine,
With laughter all around.
Each drop is a giggle,
Floating up from the ground.

Blossom's Liquid Embrace

Petals drop like cash,
In a flurry to be sweet.
A sticky summer search,
For the ultimate treat.

Jars of laughter stored,
In my pantry so bright.
Each taste a chuckle,
In the warm morning light.

Essence of the Flower's Heart

Every sip a smile,
A taste of springtime cheer.
Flowers dance and twirl,
As the sunshine draws near.

Golden drops of joy,
In the air they twine.
Flavors burst like confetti,
A sweet day, oh so fine!

Glistening Dewdrops of Delight

In gardens where the flowers sway,
A bee gets tipsy on bright play.
With each drop, a giggly buzz,
Who knew that blooms could cause such fuzz?

Frogs in joy begin to croak,
While ants do dance to a wee bit of smoke.
Drunk on sun and sweetened air,
Nature's laughter fills the fair.

Lavish Libations of Bloom

A butterfly in search of cheer,
Sips from petals, full of beer.
Coreopsis brews a golden brew,
Leaves the ladybugs tipsy too!

Bees wear crowns of nectar bliss,
As blooms toast to the morning kiss.
Each drop swirls like a merry song,
In the garden where we all belong.

Elixir of Warm Kisses

The sun pours warmth like honeyed cheer,
Kisses flying as friends appear.
With laughter sweet, a party starts,
Every bloom plays its quirky parts.

A squirrel nibbles from a cup,
While daisies sway, they lift it up.
The rabbits join in silly dance,
In a world where they take a chance.

Sips of Celestial Gold

Stars twinkle as the night unfolds,
Moonlight shimmers, purest golds.
Crickets chirp, a joyful sound,
In a sip, the cosmos found.

With each taste, a giggle shared,
Even the owls are slightly scared.
The universe sings, lively and bold,
As we sip on dreams wrapped in gold.

Drifting on a Breeze of Savor

A bee in a bowtie, how dapper he flies,
With pollen-packed pockets, he's quite the surprise.
He dances on flowers, a whimsical sight,
Buzzing out jokes, from morning till night.

The sweetness he gathers is grand and immense,
While rocking a smile that makes perfect sense.
With humor so rich, he cracks wise with glee,
In the garden of giggles, where everyone's free.

Petal Phrases and Winged Whispers

A butterfly whispers, 'You're looking quite fly!'
To a daisy who blushes, like, 'Oh my, oh my!'
The humor in blooms is a blooming delight,
Where petals spin tales in the warm morning light.

The caterpillar chuckles, 'I'll join the parade!'
In a party of puns that the sun has arrayed.
With laughter they flutter, in colors each day,
In a world made of whimsy, come swing, come play!

Time Spent in Fragrant Reverie

In the midst of the blossoms, a squirrel takes a snack,
With crumbs on his whiskers, he's got quite the knack.
He tells all his friends, 'This snack's not a bore, '
'It's like gourmet cuisine that's just washed ashore!'

His buddies all giggle, 'Can we have a taste?'
'The berries are ripe, we must not let haste! '
They feast and they frolic, their laughter so bright,
In a haven of humor, from morning till night.

Savoring Daydreams from the Orchard

An apple rolls over, with a grin so round,
It says to the peach, 'Let's go join the sound!'
They bounce through the branches, with merriment high,
Singing sweet tunes as the breeze passes by.

The grapes form a trio, with a giggly verse,
'If we get too squished, we'll be living in curse!'
But round and playful, they sway with delight,
In a world full of laughter, they shine ever bright.

Sweetly Intertwined Moments

Buzzing bees in flight, so spry,
Chasing scent like it's pie in the sky.
Sticky hands from a summer treat,
Laughter spills from every sweet beat.

A squirrel steals my jelly from toast,
Mischief munches, that furry little ghost.
Honey drips down with a giggle and cheer,
Every sticky moment, we hold so dear.

Lilting Flavors from Nature's Altar

A berry burst, a pop of delight,
Pies and laughter dance in the night.
Silly faces smeared in jam,
Who knew fruit could cause such a slam?

The grape slid right off the picnic sheet,
Bouncing like it's got two left feet.
Nature's candy at our fingertips,
Sticky situations lead to joyful trips.

The Harmony of Nature's Bounty

Carrots sing as they play hide and seek,
While tomatoes blush, going all meek.
Lettuce whispers jokes in a breeze,
Green puns sprout like leaves on the trees.

On the swing, cucumbers giggle and sway,
Twirling around in a salad ballet.
A food fight erupts, oh what a sight,
Nature's bounty spreads joy, pure delight!

The Elixir of Garden Dreams

In the garden, magic potions brew,
Pickles jumping like they just broke through.
Lemonade rivers flow with a splash,
Freckled children run, what a dash!

Chasing butterflies, oh what a race,
While mint leaves sprout with a grin on their face.
Every snack breaks into gleeful play,
Whimsical moments fill up the day.

Glistening Moments in a Cup

A splash of joy on the edge of a mug,
A dance of bits that just wanna hug.
With every sip, the giggles grow,
Like tiny bubbles, putting on a show.

Stirring trouble in the kitchen chaos,
A spoon's a dancer in the sweet pathos.
Coffee or tea? Let's not be bland,
I'll take a glittery drink, oh isn't it grand?

Sweet Fragrances of the Earth

Whiffs of mischief float in the air,
Flowers plotting a fragrant affair.
Bees are buzzing, they wear a grin,
Gathering trouble, let the fun begin!

Under petals, secrets hide,
Busy bugs on a wild ride.
With each bloom, the laughter swells,
Nature's pranksters with stories to tell.

Bright Petals in a Glass

A vase of laughter on the counter stands,
Petals waving their tiny hands.
"Look at us!" they seem to shout,
Colorful jokes they can't live without.

Sipping sunshine from a flowered brew,
With goofy grins, the petals grew.
Laughter spilled on the tabletop,
As blooms and giggles decided to hop.

Liquid Poetry of the Garden

In the garden where rivers twist,
Liquid lines with a playful mist.
A splash of verse in every drop,
Funny tales that never stop.

Raindrops laughing on thirsty leaves,
Jokes in puddles that the garden weaves.
Sip the sunlight and dance a bit,
Where quirky poetry finds its split.

Vibrant Flavors of Sunrise

A splash of orange, a twist of lime,
A drink so bright, it dances in rhyme.
Sipping on sunshine, feeling so bold,
With every gulp, my stories unfold.

The berries giggle, the mango sings,
Each sip I take, my laughter springs.
It's a carnival party in a glass so wide,
Join the fun ride, take a taste inside!

The Golden Essence in Glass

Bees buzz around like they've lost their minds,
Chasing sweet drops that none of us find.
A straw like a rocket, I slurp with a cheer,
While onlookers wonder, 'What's going on here?'

The gold in my drink is a treasure, it seems,
Mixing with laughter, confetti, and dreams.
Clinking my glass with a wink and a nod,
Cheers to the chaos—oh, isn't it odd?

Enchanted Sips of Surreal Calm

A whisper of mint in a bubble of bliss,
I took a big gulp and then went amiss.
Spinning in circles like a dizzy old fool,
Who knew that calm could be so uncool?

Floating in flavors from another plain,
I'm sipping unicorns—wait, was that a train?
With every swig, my worries take flight,
Living the daydream, oh, what a delight!

Garden's Kiss in Every Drop

Petals and pollen go swirling about,
Like a parade where everyone shouts.
Bottled sunbeams in hues oh so sweet,
With every taste, it's a floral retreat.

Lemonade daisies and lavender dreams,
Feeling so happy, bursting at the seams.
The garden's alive with a giggle and cheer,
Each sip says, 'Stay! You're welcome here!'

Fruity Echoes in the Air

In the summer sun, berries burst,
Juicy jokes, quenching our thirst.
Lemonade laughs, so refreshing and bright,
Watermelon giggles, pure delight.

Bananas slipping on the ground,
Tropical mischief all around.
Peaches whisper, secrets they keep,
While grapefruits tumble in a heap.

Liquid Garden Bliss

Sipping sunshine, with strawberries near,
Giggling vines, bring good cheer.
Cucumber jokes in the punch bowl swim,
Mint leaves dance, on a whim.

Tomato tunes, a savory song,
With basil companions, nothing can go wrong.
Cherries chuckle, on top of the drink,
As pickles ponder, and start to think.

Aroma of Sweet Rejuvenation

Honeyed breezes through the door,
Little bees buzzing, always wanting more.
Sugar cubes prance, candied delight,
As syrupy smiles shine so bright.

Marshmallow clouds float in the air,
Gummy bears gather, in little pairs.
Brownie bites hold a secret laugh,
While frosting blunders on a half.

Embrace of Floral Essence

Petal puns tickle the nose,
In gardens where the laughter grows.
Violets giggle in purple hues,
Daisies whisper with the morning dews.

Rosewater showers, a laugh in disguise,
While pansies wink with playful eyes.
Lavender dreams drift softly about,
With dandelions puffing, there's no doubt.

Whimsical Whispers of Liquid Gold

In a garden filled with giggles bright,
Buzzing pals take their flight.
Sipping sweetness, oh what a sight,
A dance of joy from morning light.

Bees wear tiny hats, so dapper and neat,
Juggling petals, they can't be beat.
With every drop, their tiny hearts greet,
Their liquid laughter makes life sweet.

A sticky debate on flavor so bold,
Cherry kisses or lemony gold?
They argue and flit, stories unfold,
Chasing flavors that never get old.

So sip the sunshine, take a chance,
Join the bees for a silly dance.
With every drizzle, spark a romance,
Oh, life's a party in this sweet expanse.

Caresses of Flowery Essence

Under blooms where scents collide,
Sneaky squirrels try to hide.
Whiffs of candy on the slide,
Nature's pranks, with joy they ride.

Rabbits gossip, ears all a-flop,
"Did you taste that, or just hop?"
The sweetness makes everyone stop,
While flowers giggle, they can't swap.

Hummingbirds in tuxedos sway,
Sipping treats while they play.
With every buzz, they brighten the day,
Dressed to impress in their ballet.

So laugh with petals, dance a spree,
The world's a flower, wild and free.
In our cups, let's sip with glee,
Where funny friendships always be.

Cascade of Sugared Memories

In a jar of sunshine, things get sticky,
Lollipops giggle and marshmallows are picky.
A gummy bear waltzes, what a sight,
Chocolate frogs croak, bringing pure delight.

Mints in the corner, whispering jokes,
Candy-coated secrets shared by the folks.
A piñata blushes, filled with confetti,
While licorice laughs at being so petty.

Jellybeans jump around with glee,
Each flavor a riddle, come unwrap and see!
Sugary sprinkles fall from above,
Creating sweet memories, all wrapped in love.

The Alchemy of Flavor and Bloom

In a cauldron of flavors, we stir and we mix,
With gummy worms dancing, pulling their tricks.
A sprinkle of sugar, a dash of pure fun,
Turning sour frowns into giggles, they run.

Cocoa clouds frolic and whip up some cream,
Whipped up a whirlwind, crafting a dream.
Unicorns sip rainbows from cups full of cheer,
Creating a buzz that sweetens the air.

Syrups are plotting with jellies in tow,
Marshmallow mischief in a whimsical show.
Each sip a journey, each bite a surprise,
With smiles and laughter that never says goodbye.

Aroma of Morning Dew

Awake with the dawn, the syrupy breeze,
Maple trees chuckle, shaking their leaves.
A pancake flip flops, it's played in the sun,
While waffles giggle, their battle's just begun.

Honey bees buzz with a sweet little grin,
Stirring up giggles from deep down within.
A morning toast dances, feeling quite grand,
With marmalade giggling, it waves from the stand.

Orange zest chuckles, it's bright and it sings,
Jams making promises with all of their flings.
In this breakfast circus, a playful delight,
Every flavor's a friend, making mornings feel right.

Transcendent Brews of Bliss

A teapot whistles with giggles and steam,
While chamomile dreams join a cozy team.
Espresso beans waltz in a caffeinated race,
Creating a buzz that's hard to replace.

Lavender sips with a pinch of a laugh,
Joking with honey, sharing a sweet half.
The froth art is giggling, it's drawn with a swirl,
Coffee cups dance, oh such a merry whirl.

Fragrant spices twirl, painting portraits in air,
While mints make a mockery of bitter despair.
Each drop is a story, each sip is a cheer,
In this world of brews, joy's always near.

Sipping Secrets of the Hive

In the hive, a buzzing spree,
Honey drips, oh joy, and glee!
Bees with glasses, sipping slow,
Plans for parties, don't you know?

Tiny wings and tiny bites,
Dancing round in bright delights.
They mix and mingle, sweetly sly,
Winks of honey, oh my, oh my!

With jars aplenty, they take a chance,
Sweetest game of waggle dance.
Stirring potions, oh what fun,
Each new flavor, just begun!

Laughter echoes through the air,
Sticky fingers everywhere.
With every sip, a hearty cheer,
Buzzing secrets, sweet and clear!

Serene Savorings at Twilight

Evening falls with golden hues,
Bees are sipping, sharing news.
Chillin' out with floral sips,
Whispers sweet and buzzing quips.

Moonlight beams on stick and straw,
They clink their flutes with a little awe.
A sip of lavender, maybe thyme,
"Cheers to bees!"—a sip sublime.

While flowers snooze, the tales unfold,
Of summer days and petals bold.
Jokes abound, and spirits high,
"Who's buzzing loud? Oh, that's just I!"

As night unfolds, the stars appear,
Their drinks are full, they have no fear.
In sips of joy, they find their place,
A honeyed smile on every face!

The Brew of Nature's Delights

From blooms to bottles, look at that!
Mixing up a fizz with chat.
Sipping on sunshine, a funny spree,
"Today I blend hibiscus tea!"

Bees wearing shades and silly hats,
Claiming sips, discussing chats.
"Is it citrus, berry, or mint?
I'll drink it all, I've no hint!"

In a cauldron, they stir and swish,
Cucumber slices, a bee's dear wish.
Each concoction garnished sweet,
Buzzing laughter on repeat.

At garden parties, they gather round,
With every swig, they dance and bound.
Nature's brew, oh what a night!
Buzzing joys and bubbly light!

Lush Liquid Melodies

Sippin' on sweet serenades,
Bees composing in sunlit glades.
Pollens mixing in a song,
Sipping softly, all day long.

In the hollow of a flower cup,
They gather 'round, and drink it up.
"Is this a tune, or just a buzz?
Let's sip some more, just because!"

Notes of citrus swirl and rise,
While floral laughter fills the skies.
Playing flutes with tiny straws,
"Bees are the best!"—their prompt applause.

With every sip, a little giggle,
Dancing wings, a joyful wiggle.
Conducting tunes from blooms so fair,
Nature's nectar fills the air!

The Allure of Gathered Ambrosia

Buzzing bees take a break,
Sipping sweetness made of cake.
They dance with joy on daisy tops,
Hoping their honey never stops.

A jar of glee, a sticky treat,
Every spoonful feels like a cheat.
Laughter spills, it drips and rolls,
Oh, the fun in sticky bowls!

Was that a fly? Or just a prank?
A funny face and a sweet thank.
With laughter shared in sunny rays,
We savor life on silly days.

So if you see a bee mid-flight,
Join the dance, it feels so right.
Gather 'round with friends so dear,
Toast your jars and share some cheer!

Mellow Moments in Blooming Meadows

A flower whispers, 'Come and play!'
The grass is soft, and here we stay.
We stumble, trip, and laugh out loud,
Amongst the blooms, we're quite the crowd.

A picnic spread of funny snacks,
Sandwiches with silly cracks.
We giggle at the ants' parade,
As crumbs of joy are lightly laid.

The sun dips low, a yellow glow,
We chase the shadows, to and fro.
Each flower nods in pure delight,
As laughter fills the mellow night.

So grab a bloom, and let it sway,
In blooming meadows, fun's the way.
Convert the mundane, shake your frown,
In this fine field, we're all renown!

Chromatic Flavors of the Spring

Colors burst like laughter bright,
Flavors twirl in pure delight.
A purple sip, a yellow taste,
In this wonder, none to waste.

Berries jiggle on a plate,
A fruit dance that feels quite great.
Cherry pops and lemon zings,
We munch and crunch; oh, the joy it brings!

With every bite, a giggle's sound,
Each flavor makes the world go round.
We paint our faces with the hue,
In this spring fling, there's fun for two.

So raise your glass to zestful sway,
Let's mix the colors, play all day!
In this riot of flavors, join the spree,
For laughter blooms, so wild and free!

Tasting the Blossoms' Farewell

As petals fall like confetti sweet,
We taste the air, a summery treat.
The floral dance begins to sway,
In this farewell, we laugh and play.

A red bloom falls right on my nose,
What a sight, oh, how it shows!
With every breeze, a giggle flies,
As nature's prankster plays disguise.

Gone are the blooms, but not our cheer,
We celebrate the end, my dear.
With flavors bold, and laughter swell,
In this farewell, we wish them well.

So raise a glass to petals past,
Let's toast the moments, make them last.
In every end, there's fun to find,
In tasting life, we're always kind!

Serenading the Sweets of Summer

A bee in the garden sings loud,
Its buzz makes the flowers feel proud.
With a wink and a joke, it does sway,
Turning sunlight to fun every day.

The fruits are juggling, what a sight,
While the sun plays tag with the night.
Watermelons giggle, oh such glee,
Sharing secrets with the bright honey bee.

Picnics abound with laughter and cheer,
As ants march in line, they cheerfully steer.
Chasing crumbs in a musical dance,
Who knew a sandwich could lead to romance?

So raise a glass to the days of delight,
To sweet little moments that feel so right.
With each drop of joy, let's sing loud,
In the garden of life, we're all quite proud.

A Journey Through Floral Fantasies

In a world where petunias wear hats,
And sunflowers dance with the acrobats.
Every rose has a story to share,
Whispering secrets of love in the air.

Lilies wear sunglasses, oh what a sight,
As daisies throw petals in pure delight.
The tulips tap dance on snazzy heels,
Making their wishes on daffodil reels.

Butterflies flutter, they all have flair,
Discussing the day over lemonade fair.
While the violets crack jokes with the thyme,
Creating a garden that's simply sublime.

So come, take a stroll through this dream,
Where every bloom has a laugh and a theme.
In this floral parade of whimsical cheer,
Life's little pleasures become crystal clear.

Sweet Symphony of Sips

There's a punch bowl filled with giggles at noon,
As lemons and limes sing a sunny tune.
Straws like snorkels dive into fun,
Every sip's a burst of cheer on the run.

Coconut whispers its tropical tales,
While berries sparkle, catching the gales.
Ice cubes clatter, they sing when they fall,
In a symphony of laughter, a liquid brawl.

Mint leaves are dancing, they shake with finesse,
Each drink a party, can't settle for less.
The punchline's delicious, it's quite a play,
As we sip all our worries and troubles away.

So clink those cups, let's raise a cheer,
To flavors and fun that bring us near.
A toast to our laughter, so sweet and divine,
In this bubbly adventure, we're all feeling fine.

Golden Elixirs at Dusk

As the sun dips low, a glow in the glass,
Golden liquids sparkle, making us laugh.
With a wink and a nod, they beckon and tease,
Turning the mundane into joyous ease.

There's ginger with spice, oh what a kick,
In this evening potion, it's quite the trick.
Lemonade listens to stories of old,
While mischief gets bottled, a sight to behold.

Carafes filled with giggles and dreams,
Bubbling with sweetness, bursting at the seams.
The ice clinks a tune, the flavors collide,
In this dusky hour, let's set joys aside.

So share a toast to the nightfall's delight,
With elixirs of laughter to warm up the night.
In this golden glow, we gather and cheer,
For the magic that sparkles when friends are near.

A Cascade of Golden Delights

In a jar that's sticky and full,
A bee took a dive, looking for a pull.
He slipped on a flower, spun around,
Said, 'This sweet stuff should be renowned!'

The apples were laughing, all in a row,
'Why so serious? Just let it flow!'
A squirrel piped up, with a nut in his paw,
'Join our feast or you'll be in awe!'

Sunshine dripped from the tree's embrace,
While a honeycomb did a little jiggy grace.
The fruits tossed seeds like a party trick,
Hoping to grow another citrus click!

So let's toast to the mishaps of buzz,
For gold on the tongue makes any heart fuzz.
What a hoot it is to just take a chance,
With a splash of sweetness, let's break into dance!

Poetry Brewed in the Meadow

In a meadow where daisies wear hats,
A frog recited poems to curious cats.
They nodded along, with eyes oh so wide,
While sipping on dew, side by side.

A butterfly fluffed his colorful wings,
'Why talk of troubles when laughter sings?'
And a beetle replied with a chuckle so deep,
'Let's make rhymes that'll tickle our sleep!'

Breezes danced, tickling petals all around,
Each whisper brought giggles, a joyful sound.
While ants marched in lines, a parade they declared,
With tiny trumpets, they proudly shared!

So let's gather 'round for a verse or two,
With bugs and blooms in this charming view.
In the meadow where silliness reigns supreme,
We'll write our laughter, it's truly a dream!

Sweet Secrets of the Wild

In a forest where trees gossip with glee,
A raccoon gave secrets with mischievous spree.
'Taste the berries, they'll make you sing,
Just avoid the prickles—oh, that stings!'

A curious fox with a flair for fun,
Joined the party under the sunny run.
'With honey on toast, and acorns on the side,
Let's munch till we wobble! Let's enjoy the ride!'

A parrot squawked tales of glorious feasts,
While squirrels debated the fluffiest treats.
Each bite of the wild was a tickle to know,
With flavors so crazy, they just had to flow!

So dive into this feast that nature provides,
With giggles and grins, let our appetite ride.
In the wild where the silly guarantees fun,
We'll dance, we'll feast, till the day's finally done!

The Language of Blooming Fruits

In orchards where laughter hangs from the trees,
Fruit spoke in riddles, dipping just like a breeze.
'An apple a day can chase blues far away,
But it's more fun to laugh, what do you say?'

The peaches were plump, with juice overflowing,
While cherries chimed in with a giggly showing.
'Let's create a party, mix colors so bright,
Our sweetness combined, oh what a delight!'

A grape bounced around, with a fibersome dance,
'The trick is to roll for a juicy romance!'
While bananas split jokes that made others snicker,
Chortling till twilight, their humor was quicker.

So gather your fruit, let the flavors collide,
With laughter and joy that we just can't hide.
In this orchard of giggles, together we'll sing,
The language of fruits is a heartening ring!

The Melodic Flavor of Flora

In gardens where the flowers laugh,
Bees dance around like they're on a path.
They sip and swirl, with funny grace,
A sweet ballet in nature's embrace.

The daisies gossip with the breeze,
While tulips tease with wiggly knees.
The buzzing bees wear tiny hats,
Playing croquet with clueless cats.

Hummingbirds sing a zippy tune,
As if they're sponsored by the moon.
Around the petals, a wacky fuss,
Like a wild party, just for us.

So raise your cup to plant-based cheer,
With every sip, the jests draw near.
Flora's flavor, a grand delight,
Let's toast to giggles, day and night.

Sips from Nature's Cauldron

In a kettle brewed with flower flakes,
Mirth bubbles up in swirling lakes.
Sip your teacup, watch it hop,
The laughter's strong, it just won't stop.

With every pour, the petals sing,
A funny tune in the springy fling.
The herbs are stirring, making jokes,
Telling tales of the sneaky oaks.

Lemonade from sun-kissed blooms,
Giggles fill the garden rooms.
The honey's sticky, laughter flows,
More amusing than a circus show.

So come on down and take a drink,
Nature's brew is here to link.
With every sip, joy's in the air,
In this cauldron, find humor rare.

The Reverie of Golden Drops

Golden drops from petals spill,
A sweet surprise, a thrilling thrill.
Collecting drops is quite the game,
Laughter echoes, nobody's tame.

The wind is writing silly rhymes,
While nature's clock is slow with chimes.
Honeyed whispers float around,
In this garden, joy is found.

Sunshine mingles with giggles bright,
As creatures join in pure delight.
Bumblebees in tiny shorts,
Practicing for their buzzing sports.

So fill your glass with liquid gold,
Sip the fun that never gets old.
Each drop a chuckle, a cheerful cheer,
Nature's comedy is always near.

Brewed Verses of the Earth

With roots that twist and leaves that smile,
We gather here for fun awhile.
This brew of laughter, robust and bold,
Insights and antics waiting to unfold.

Plant puns scatter through the air,
The flowers giggle, without a care.
Roses boast of their sweet charm,
But daisies quip, "We have the calm!"

Each sip brings jokes from leafy friends,
With wacky tales that never ends.
In this cup, the earth has spun,
As we toast to laughter, all in fun.

So raise your mug to every sprout,
In this wild world, there's never doubt.
Let's drink from life's abundant cup,
And share the laughter—never stop!

Elixirs of the Heart

In a bottle, love is stored,
Like raspberry jam, it can be poured.
Sip too fast, you'll start to grin,
Watch out now, it may begin!

Lemon zest and honey's sway,
Mixing laughter in the fray.
Tickle your tongue with a burst of cheer,
Third cup in, we have no fear!

Chocolate dreams and fizzy glee,
Dancing taste buds, wild and free.
Sip a little, spill some too,
Oops! That was meant for you!

With each gulp, a giggle spills,
Taste the chaos, feel the thrills.
Pouring joy in every glass,
In this brew, let's raise our sass!

Buzzing Beneath the Petals

Under blooms, a party flows,
Butterflies toss aside their woes.
Drinks that shimmer, colors bright,
Let's mix and laugh under the light.

A splash of fancy, a dash of fun,
Pour me a drink, let's not be done!
Bees are humming a jolly tune,
Swirling around our paper moon.

Grinning daisies nod in sync,
Join us now, don't you blink!
Sipping sweet, we avoid the sting,
In this garden, let joy ring!

Charming sips with silliness abound,
Life's elixirs circle round.
Buzz like bees, bounce like spring,
A sip of life makes our hearts sing!

Liquid Sunshine on My Tongue

A citrus burst, bright as day,
Wakes my senses, come what may.
Fancy flavors, zesty dreams,
Sipping sunshine, or so it seems.

With every drop, a giggle grows,
Lemonade rivers, who even knows?
Toast the ruin of my best laid plans,
Gulping joy with friendly clans.

Pineapple hula dances in a cup,
Tropical flavors, fill me up!
Straws like rocket ships take flight,
In every sip, pure delight!

Orange bubbles race on by,
I'm the captain—let's all fly!
Drink it down, let worries bob,
Liquid sunshine, that's my job!

Harvesting the Taste of Life

In the orchard, choice fruits sway,
Grab a vessel, come what may.
Ripe and ready, berry bliss,
A sip of joy? Oh, do not miss!

Whisking giggles into a brew,
Lively concoctions, how about you?
First sip tickles, second makes me grin,
Careful now, let the fun begin!

Crimson cherries chase the gloom,
Let's dance around, make some room.
With every taste, a laughter sprout,
This joy-filled glass is what it's about!

Harvesting sweetness in the day,
Bubbling laughter, come what may.
Pour your heart and take a chance,
In this life, we twirl and dance!

A Symphony of Sugared Breezes

In fields where bees conspire to play,
Buzzing whimsies dance all day.
With syrups stuck on every wing,
They giggle as they sip and sing.

Bright blossoms offer sweet delight,
A taste of giggles, pure and bright.
They try to stash their load in vain,
Oh how they bumble, what a gain!

The sunbeam's laughter, oh so sweet,
It tickles petals, makes them fleet.
A flute of flowers, jolly sounds,
As happy chaos twirls around.

So join the frolic, don't be shy,
Let pollen tickle, let hearts fly.
In this sweet opera, full of cheer,
Every laugh's a burst of nectar here.

The Poetry of Pollen and Light

A dandelion's wish takes flight,
Floating softly, pure delight.
Little drifters dance on air,
Spreading giggles everywhere.

With sun-kissed rays that gleam and play,
The flower's winks make poets sway.
Each petal's blush and playful tease,
Composes joy with every breeze.

The bumblebee croons a silly tune,
It's happy hour, never too soon.
While daisies roll in grassy beds,
They share their jokes, sprinkle their threads.

Oh, frothy blooms in wild display,
Crack jokes that make the blossoms sway.
In nature's rhyme, we find our cheer,
With every giggle growing near.

Embrace of the Floral Essence

In gardens where the colors clash,
Petal parties share a splash.
A tulip trips, a rose looks sly,
"Hey, watch me shine!" they laugh and cry.

With fragrant hugs, the blossoms greet,
Pollinators tap their tiny feet.
The violets boast in purple pride,
Whispering secrets, what a ride!

Sunbeams tickle, light delight,
They chase the shadows, morning bright.
Each flower's grin is wide and wild,
A goofy dance, nature's child.

So twirl along in this floral spree,
Let giggles echo, set them free.
In hues of humor, let us blend,
The bloom of laughter never ends.

Beneath the Veil of Petals

Under petals, secrets sneak,
Each bloom a gossip, full of cheek.
They whisper tales, both bright and bold,
As insects laugh and share their gold.

A lily's waltz, a daisy's prance,
Each flower knows how to enhance.
With pollen trails and silly squawks,
They paint the world with joyous talks.

In a garden circus, blooms abound,
Flowers juggling laughs all around.
A poppy slips, oh what a fall,
They giggle loud, "Come one, come all!"

So lean in close, join the cheer,
Nature's laughter, oh so clear.
Beneath those petals, fun awaits,
A riot of joy from nature's traits.

A Dance of Dripping Gold

In a jar with a twisty lid,
A sweet dance begins, oh so hid.
Bees buzz around in perfect glee,
Sticky fingers, that's just me!

I spread it thick on my toasted bread,
Honey drips down, oh what a spread!
Critters gather, it's a grand buffet,
I wave my arms, shoo them away!

With every drop, a giggle escapes,
This liquid gold makes funny shapes.
I took a sip, lost my balance,
Spinning 'round like it's a dance!

So when life gives you sweet surprises,
Dance with joy, undisguises!
Messy hands and a silly grin,
Means another round, let the fun begin!

Infusions of Earthly Joy

A splash of color, a hint of zest,
Every sip is a cheerful jest.
I blend and mix, a fruity mess,
Taste testers laugh, I must confess!

Upside down, in my favorite bowl,
Fruits collide, they take a stroll.
A sip of laughter, a dash of cheer,
Who knew joy could come in here?

With every taste, I feel the thrill,
A giggle-potion, what a skill!
Friends gather 'round, we cheer and shout,
What else is life, but a laugh-out-loud!

So stir and blend, let the flavors play,
A banquet of joy, come what may.
In every bubble, a chuckle awaits,
Infusions of cheer on our plates!

Liquid Sunshine on My Lips

Oh what's this bottle, bright and bold?
A golden potion, pure liquid gold!
With a twist and a pop, I take a swig,
The taste is wild, makes me jig!

Sunshine bubbles up, a frothy wave,
Just like laughter, sweet and brave.
Friends around, we sip and spill,
Giggling hard, we can't keep still!

A splash on my nose, a squirt on my chin,
Laughter erupts, oh what a win!
A toast to blunders, we cheer and clap,
Sloshy fun, in a sticky trap!

So pucker up, let the bubbles burst!
In every sip, we quench our thirst.
Liquid sunshine, a sip from the skies,
With every laugh, our spirits rise!

The Sugar of Sunlit Petals

A drizzle here, a sprinkle there,
Petals dance without a care.
I taste the sweetness, oh so bright,
A sugary giggle, pure delight!

Crunchy leaves, they crinkle and crack,
Sipping nectar makes me wack.
I twirl 'round with petals in hand,
Creating chaos that's simply grand!

Friends gather close for the flower feast,
Each sip ignites a funny beast.
A swish and a splash, laughter ignites,
Turns every moment into wild flights!

So here's to petals, sweet and fine,
Poured in cups, a life divine.
With giggles and joy, let's make a toast,
For sweetened moments we love the most!

Floral Floods of Flavor

In the garden, bees take flight,
Sipping secrets, oh what a sight!
Tasting flowers from dawn till dusk,
That honeycomb's more than just musk.

Petals giggle as they sway,
Whispers of sweet in a playful way.
A daisy dance, quite the charade,
Buzzing, laughing, they serenade.

Butterflies join the grand parade,
Wings so bright, they won't degrade.
Chasing liquids, licking thrills,
Nature's joy, it fills, it fills!

In floral floods, let's toast our cheer,
With every laugh, and every beer.
Let's sip from blooms 'til skies turn dark,
And celebrate with light and spark!

Nectarous Melodies in the Breeze

A buzzing symphony fills the air,
Flowers giggle without a care.
Leaves are tapping to the beat,
Nature's choir, quite a treat!

Sipping sunshine from petals wide,
Fancy flavors on a ride.
With every sip, a silly grin,
A bouquet of chuckles deep within.

The wind's a jokester, full of pranks,
It flips my hat, then laughs, then thanks.
Each gust carries laughter's call,
As blooms bounce and gusts enthrall.

Dance, oh blooms, in vibrant hues,
With every sip, let's drink the blues.
A joyful chorus, sweet and bright,
In midday sun, we sip, we bite!

Moonlit Drops of Sweetness

Under starlight, laughter glows,
Sipping sweetness where the moon throws.
Liquid laughter from blossoms fair,
Smiles abound in the night air.

Fireflies flicker, join the fun,
Chasing flavors, isn't it spun?
Sipping stars in sparkling beams,
Where every drop stirs wacky dreams.

Moonbeams tickle, it's plain to see,
As we share this sugary spree.
Each taste a giggle, each sip a cheer,
Filling nights with fun and beer.

In this dance of whimsy and sweets,
We'll toast with joy, oh, what a feast!
With drops of sweetness, laughter flows,
Moonlit moments, the heart knows!

The Spellbinding Sip

A potion brewed of colors bright,
With every sip, oh what a sight!
Magic in a cup, cheers all around,
With chuckles blooming, laughter's found.

Wands made of straws stir up delight,
With every slurp, we take flight.
Bubbles rise, casting silly spells,
In every gulp, the joy swells.

Flavors dancing, twirls and leaps,
In this chalice, enchantment sleeps.
Sipping giggles, casting cheer,
In our cups, the magic's here!

So raise a glass, join the show,
With every sip, let laughter flow.
Where sweet concoctions spark the light,
In spellbinding sips, we unite!

Whispers of Honeyed Dreams

In fields where bees do dance and sway,
They steal our snacks and fly away.
With sticky paws and tiny feet,
They buzz about, oh what a treat!

A spoonful drops, a golden glow,
The ants all come to steal the show.
A comedy of munch and crunch,
Their sweet parade, a sticky brunch!

The flowers blush as bees arrive,
With pollen backpacks, oh how they thrive!
They mischief around, what a ruckus!
I guess this buzz is quite contagious!

In dreams, they chatter, sip and sip,
Driving 'round on sticky zip.
A playful buzz, the whole night through,
Who knew bees were such jesters too?

Sipping on Sunlit Bliss

A cat on a windowsill so bright,
Sips sunbeams, feeling just right.
It dreams of milk and rivers of gold,
Chasing those rays, so fearless and bold!

A lazy dog sprawled out on the lawn,
Sips lemonade in the break of dawn.
It wags its tail with the sweetest sound,
Living the good life, just rolling around!

A bumblebee playing hopscotch in air,
Buzzing with joy without a care.
It lands in flowers, a tipsy spree,
Filling the day with giggles and glee!

As we sip our joy from sunny cups,
The silly critters fill our ups.
With laughter and cheer, we share a toast,
To all the fun that we love the most!

The Sweetest Lullabies of Nature

In the garden, the flowers softly croon,
A lullaby sung to the evening moon.
The crickets chirp, a serenade sweet,
While the frogs join in with a funky beat!

The trees whisper secrets, the wind's gentle tease,
While ants do a waltz with the honeyed breeze.
Fireflies twinkle, like stars in a row,
Dancing to rhythms only they know!

The breezes giggle, the blossoms sway,
As butterflies twirl in joyous play.
Each note they share, a charm on the air,
Brings smiles to faces, erasing all care!

So listen closely, let your worries float,
On nature's tunes, we'll lazily gloat.
With each sweet note, a laugh will bloom,
In this whimsical world, there's always room!

Fragrant Moments in Bloom

The daisies dance in their polka-dot clothes,
With petals that giggle, heaven knows!
The daffodils chuckle, oh what a sight,
Joining the party, from day into night!

The roses blush, in lipstick red,
Tickling the bees as they wander ahead.
The lilies whisper whimsical tales,
While piñatas of pollen float on the gales!

With sun-kissed cheeks, the garden's alive,
Creating a circus where laughter can thrive.
Bouncing about like a joyful balloon,
In this fragrant fair, we're all over the moon!

So let's raise a toast to the petals that play,
In this bloom of mirth, let worries decay.
With every sweet moment, let joy take its flight,
In the fragrant embrace of nature's delight!

The Bounty on The Tongue

In the garden, what a sight,
Flowers giggle, hold on tight.
Bees are buzzing, do they know?
Stocks are high in sugary flow.

Marmalade suns and candy vines,
Sipping sweetness, oh how divine!
Taste of laughter, sip of cheer,
Lollipops rain when friends are near.

Fruit in laughter, golden hue,
Nature's jester, playful too.
Grapes like jokes, wine with a pun,
Who knew life's a sugar run?

With a wink, petals sway,
Sweets gathered at the end of the day.
Lemon zings with a zesty laugh,
Living life like candy craft!

Sweets from the Botanist's Past

A botanist's dreams, oh what a tale,
Jars of jam and licorice grail.
Old recipes made with a wink,
Stir into laughter, don't even think!

Pickled petals, what a treat,
Dancing flavors, oh so sweet!
Chutney giggles in every spread,
Workers whisper, 'Is that bread?'

Pollen parties on a sunny day,
Flavored sunshine in wild array.
Smiles whisked in nectar cups,
Forget the diet, fill 'er up!

Delicious chaos, blend of cheer,
Drizzled honey, no room for fear.
A smear of bliss on your dish,
Taste the fun, fulfill that wish!

Echoes of Sugared Blooms

In the garden, laughter spills,
Petals chatter, joy that thrills.
Jellybeans fall from the trees,
Nature's humor, playful breeze.

Fluffy clouds of cotton candy,
Swaying flowers, oh so dandy!
Bumblebees dance, a buzzing song,
In this world, nothing seems wrong.

Taffy vines twist and turn,
Young and old, let laughter churn.
Cherry blossoms dip and twirl,
A sugary fest in every swirl.

A breeze of mint, a splash of zest,
Every bite is a wacky quest.
In a field of bliss we roam,
Frolic and feast—we're right at home!

The Serenade of Nature's Gifts

In a meadow, joy unfolds,
Nature's gifts, a sight of gold.
Lemonade rivers, sunbeam rays,
Tickling toes in sugary ways.

Lemon-lime laugh, a fizzle, a pop,
Fruits in hats begin to hop.
Gleeful greens, with smiles wide,
Sassy fruits, they just won't hide!

Under trees, jellies collide,
We share sweet secrets, side by side.
With every sunrise, laughter flows,
In this garden where joy grows.

Sprinkle of joy, a glimmer of fun,
Gather close, the day's just begun!
Nature's humor in every bite,
Dance with glee till the fall of night!

The Charms of Floral Fusion

Petals dance in a sunny glass,
Bees buzzing, wings go 'zippity-zap.'
Lemon and lavender play tag,
Honey drips down like a sweet little trap.

Tasting flowers is quite a treat,
Giggling flavors, oh so neat!
Sipping blooms, can't take a break,
Flavorful joy, a wild cake!

Lavish ladles of silly spice,
A rainbow's worth would be quite nice.
Mixing chaos, we swirl and twirl,
Floral fun, oh what a whirl!

Who's got the fruity twist today?
Ask the daisies, they'll know the way.
Punchy petals with a hint of glee,
Let's blend in harmony, you and me!

Musical Notes of Nature's Brew

Wind sings tunes through the tall trees,
A symphony brewed with a honey tease.
Slurping laughter, take a sip,
Nature's orchestra, take a trip!

Blossoms croon with a bubbly hum,
Grapes giggle, 'Oh, what a fun!'
Citrus strums on the playful beat,
Swirling colors, oh so sweet!

In the garden, a melody plays,
Petals join in with silly ways.
Cherries chuckle, how can one stop?
Serenading flavors that just won't drop!

Lemonade leaps like a cheerful sprite,
Dancing with flavors, such pure delight.
Taste this harmony, give it a swirl,
Sipping joy in a fruit-filled whirl!

Blossoms in a Glass

Frothy tulips in a crystal cup,
Pouring petals, then drink up!
Daisies jump, lilies groove,
With every sip, the flowers move.

Sipping sunlight on a picnic spree,
Absurd flavors, who would agree?
A dash of giggles, a splash of cheer,
Floral concoctions, the fun is here!

Cups of color, swirls divine,
Roses whisper, 'Try this wine!'
Marigold mixes, give it a whirl,
Sweetened petals, come on, let's twirl!

Frolic with blossoms, raise your glass,
Each drink joined by flowers that amass.
With flavor laughter, it's quite the blast,
Let's drink to joy, let moments last!

Radiant Serendipity of Flavor

Stumbling through a garden of taste,
Lemon drops and violets, no waste.
Life's a party in each little bite,
A feast of flowers that feels so right.

A splash of whimsy in every ray,
Petal power saves the day!
Tickled by tastes, oh what a find,
Blossoming giggles, nature's kind.

Jubilant juices, colors collide,
Bubbling plants take us for a ride.
Make a toast with fruity glee,
Experience flavors wild and free!

Sipping sunshine, let's break the norm,
In a glass of fun, we transform.
With each pour, may laughter reign,
Radiant joy in every vein!

The Flavor of Distant Gardens

In the garden where gnomes eat pie,
Carrots chuckle as they grow high.
Radishes wear sunglasses, so cool,
While cabbages sit like they're in school.

Bees don their hats and dance with flair,
Honeysuckle giggles, scents in the air.
Peppers compete in spicy debates,
While tomatoes trade gossip about their mates.

Echoes of the Hummingbird's Song

A hummingbird zooms with a zoom-zoom zippity,
Sipping sweet sips, oh, what a pity!
It forgot its shades, too much shine,
Now it's dodging sunbeams like they're porcupines!

With each tiny flap, it spins a yarn,
About nectar potions from a far-off barn.
Flowers raise flags, cheering for the champ,
While daisies giggle, caught in mid-camp.

Sun-Kissed Sips from the Earth

Sunbeams flirt with the lavender bloom,
While zucchinis pose like they're in a room.
The soil murmurs secrets quite loud,
As worms wear tuxedos, feeling so proud!

Drizzle of honey makes ants do a jig,
While marigolds play tag, dancing big.
Bumblebees in bowties, what a sight,
Chasing the breeze till the afternoon's light.

In the Dance of Dews and Flowers

Dewdrops sparkle on petals, oh so fine,
While daisies do the cha-cha, feeling divine.
Butterflies twirl, granting wishes galore,
Hoping for ice cream from the garden store!

Tulips laugh as they sway to the beat,
While squirrels hopscotch in their tiny feet.
A vase of sunflowers sings silly tunes,
As frogs in the pond croak the afternoon blues.

Mellow Melodies of Sweetness

Buzzing bees with tiny tunes,
Dancing flowers in bright afternoons.
A sip from blooms, oh what a cheer,
Sweet surprises that we hold dear.

Drips and drops from petals wide,
Sticky fingers, what a ride!
Taste the laughter in the air,
Nature's candy, everywhere!

Wiggly worms on a sugar spree,
Giggling grasshoppers hop with glee.
A spoonful of sunshine, joy to share,
Mellow melodies without a care.

So raise your cups to nature's play,
Where sweetness rules both night and day.
With every sip, let worries float,
In this delicious, funny boat!

Gentle Brews of Nature's Love

A kettle whistling in the breeze,
Teapot gossip among the leaves.
Sudden splashes, a leaf's surprise,
Warm embrace, under blushing skies.

Crumbling cookies on a branch,
Squirrels join in, quick to prance.
Laughter carries with every sip,
Nature's brew gives joy a trip.

A croaking frog sings tea-time songs,
While butterflies dance, where fun belongs.
Pour another cup, let laughter flow,
In this gentle brew, let humor grow.

So raise your mugs, here's to the fun,
In nature's love, we're all as one.
Sip it slow, let joy arise,
With every brew, find no goodbyes!

Sun-Kissed Drops of Harmony

Sunshine giggles on every drop,
As fruit flies around laugh and hop.
Golden glimmers in a glass,
Join the splash, come join the class!

Frogs wear shades, sipping with flair,
While butterflies twirl without a care.
Sip of laughter, taste of fun,
Under the glow of the warming sun.

Juggling cherries, what a show!
A fruity circus, oh how they glow.
Mixing flavors, just like a song,
In this harmony, you can't go wrong!

So gather round, let's share a cheer,
For sun-kissed drops that bring us near.
Together we laugh, together we sway,
In this sweet sun, let worries stray!

Delicate Flavors of the Garden

In the garden where flavors mix,
There's a party in the unpicked sticks.
Carrots giggle, lettuce sings,
Oh the joy that freshness brings!

Tomatoes blush in the sunlight's gaze,
Cucumbers wink in their green ballet.
Every bite's a silly delight,
In this garden, all feels right.

Bees do ballet on petals bright,
Playing tag with the honeyed flight.
Sip the soup, savor that zest,
In this garden, we are blessed!

So come on down to nature's feast,
Where all the funny flavors released.
With every dish, share a grin,
In this delicate garden, let's begin!

Sweet Communion with the Earth

In gardens where the daisies dance,
I sip the sunshine, take a chance.
Bees buzzing jokes, they tickle me,
As laughter drips from every tree.

A slug slides by in snail-like grace,
Sporting shades, what a funny face!
I share my snacks with ants so small,
They party hard; they're having a ball.

Oh, how the flowers gossip bright,
Whispers of bloom in sheer delight.
A breeze that tickles every petal,
I giggle as they dance a nettle.

Under the sky, we feast and cheer,
The earth's buffet, so rich and dear.
With every bite, a chuckle found,
Together we break funny ground.

The Liquid Love Parade

Tiny drops on a leafy stage,
The plants can't help but share their rage.
A puddle winks, it pouts, it sighs,
As raindrops giggle from the skies.

Balloons of dew on blades of grass,
Chasing clouds like it's a class.
Lemonade rivers, they're bubbling sweet,
Laughter flows where two raindrops meet.

The sun's a clown in a polka-dot hat,
Sipping on drinks made from fruit and bat.
A parade of colors skips and twirls,
While flowers wink and share their pearls.

Join the dance, lift your cup high,
Where sunshine meets the welcome sky.
Though spills may happen along the way,
Who knew love could taste like play?

Petal-Infused Dreams

In dreams where petals float like fluff,
I find my thoughts are sweet enough.
A butterfly whispers, soft and bright,
Sipping honey under moonlight.

Silly things bloom in colors bold,
A marigold wearing shades of gold.
Crickets trying to sing a tune,
Lure me with magic, oh so soon!

Daisies discuss sweet secrets warm,
While tulips plot their springtime charm.
With every giggle, my heart takes flight,
In a garden where dreams feel just right.

The stars are sassy, they wink and wink,
Together we all share a drink.
In petal-infused dreams so divine,
Laughter spreads like wisps of wine.

Tasting the Whisper of the Wild

In the woods where the wild things laugh,
I sip on dew, my favorite craft.
Each berry murmurs tales so sweet,
A snack that steals both heart and seat.

Ode to the leaves, they rustle in fun,
A forest party just begun.
The squirrel jigs with a nutty grin,
While all of nature joins in the din.

I taste the breeze, it's crisp with zest,
Every wild note puts joy to the test.
With mushrooms that chuckle, oh what a scene,
Where my wild heart feels truly keen.

So raise a glass to the whispers bright,
In the wild where everything feels just right.
With every sip of joy and thrill,
I'm tasting the wild—a joyous will!

www.ingramcontent.com/pod-product-compliance
Lightning Source LLC
Chambersburg PA
CBHW051638160426
43209CB00004B/706